Essential VIRAL MARKETING Tips & Strategies For 2016 And Beyond!

For Hot Updates Follow & Tweet: @GorillaShooting Add me to the Viral Marketing List

Affiliate Invitation

Affiliates are welcome to signup for the affiliate programs that are presented in this eBook and to replace the affiliate links with your own link. Affiliates are encouraged to share this eBook freely so that it will go viral, but affiliates can also sell it and keep 100% of the commission. Registered affiliates can send email to: paladinvmdoc@gmail.com for a free editable Word doc of this eBook so you can replace the links and create a PDF eBook with your own links. Nothing can be added to this eBook and no part of it can be changed or modified except to add your affiliate links. This eBook is protected by Copyright.

Legal Notice

TABLE OF CONTENTS

1.) INTRODUCTION

The key to growth is the introduction of higher dimensions of consciousness into our awareness. via Lao Tzu

Abraham Maslow's Hierarchy of Needs

Are you sick and tired of all the hype surrounding the Internet and Viral Marketing and hearing about the next magic bullet and the new 1 click software? Do you just want the plain and simple facts that work to successfully conduct business online?

If so then you need to know that Viral Marketing has become an exact science that utilizes all of the advanced marketing strategies and digital technologies that are available. Most usually Viral Marketing refers to the promotion of ideas, knowledge, images, videos, and sounds that can be transmitted and distributed digitally. Digital transmission and distribution is the primary means by which products and information goes viral and spread like a virus from one person to the next. Although, Viral Marketing can also be used to promote physical products.

Yet, digital products have a major advantage compared to physical products because once a digital product is created it an be resold endlessly with virtually no costs by just maintaining a download link. On the other hand even the most profitable consumable products require additional inputs, labor, and resources to be manufactured again so that they can continue to be sold.

Still all that is off point about what makes a digital product become viral and exactly what is Viral Marketing. Essentially, the basic element of Viral marketing is giving the people what they like and what they want. The advanced element of Viral Marketing is to also give people what they need along with what they like and what they want.

As an example I will share findings of a Case Study on the rapper Lil' Wayne that I read while pursuing an MS in Business. In order to become rich and famous Lil' Wayne gave away (if I remember correctly) 400,000 downloads of his music. At first thought that may seem to be an unbelievably hard task, but when you consider that he would only need to produce 400 music tracks that are downloaded 1000 times it becomes a much easier task to accomplish. Then if his music was shared on social networks like Facebook and Twitter maybe his music only needed to be downloaded 200 times per day on 5 networks for a few months to go viral.

No matter how Lil' Wayne did it, the fact is, he gave the people what they like and what they want to get his first contract and become rich and famous. Being a film/video guy I tend to focus on case studies related to success in the media business. But no doubt more recently MBA programs all around the world are focused on case studies related to Psy who made the Gang Nam Style song. Psy became rich and famous by giving away 3.2 BILLION views on Youtube to break the world record. Psy gave people what they like and what they want; a great dance, colors & contrasts, beats, humor, shock, awe, and even homosexuality & most importantly he also used the latest technology.

You are probably not in the media business and wondering why or how that's relevant. The point is that no matter what industry you may be in, people make products and things go viral, so you must give people what they like and what they want to be successful at Viral Marketing. In the long term, you must also give people what they need, and they will like and care about you more. Or after the viral buzz is gone you may find business profits or popularity waning as it seems to be for Lil' Wayne & Psy.

2.) SKIPPING THE BASICS

Idealists foolish enough to throw caution to the winds have advanced mankind and have enriched the world. via Emma Goldman

Fortunately, unlike space technology the cost to implement Viral Marketing campaigns on the Internet is very inexpensive if done properly. You would easily spend thousands of dollars conducting radio and print marketing campaigns that can be done on the Internet more effectively for hundreds of dollars. For instance, new training is available that will allow you to run ads on Facebook and get website clicks and the email addresses of your visitors for less than 1 cent each:

http://www.fbtrafficninja.com/pro

Later in this eBook we will also share new software technology, that makes Viral Marketing easier than ever. The tide is rapidly turning and the big studios, publishers, and distributors no longer have a monopoly or strangle hold on small businesses and independent operators any longer. Book stores are closing, Major Newspapers & DVD rentals franchises like Block Buster are going out of business. Technology is developing rapidly.

Now a person who spent hundreds of dollars on a cellphone can get some shots that are just as good as the shots I get with the movie camera I paid thousands of dollars to buy.

Even major social networks like Facebook and advertisers like Perfect Audience and AdRroll are under attack and will need to change their business models because this is now a buyers market. Now there is Blabb and Twitter has launched Periscope, that are new technologies which allow small businesses and independent operators to directly connect with consumers in real time.

Also new software enables pc users to do things only major corporations with networked computers could do few years ago. The big Internet business bullies are losing their dominance over the marketplace, to a large extent because Viral Marketing is inexpensive and relatively easy for anyone to implement. Twitter seems to be the first major player to give lip service with it's apology to developers and promise to be more responsive and considerate, but so far it seems to be the same old story for small businesses and independent operators.

Until the end of October, 2015 there was no word from two major players, that seemed to be sitting quietly on the sidelines. Then Google/Youtube announced a portal for podcastors: https://g.co/podcastportal Possibly Microsoft/Bing/Yahoo will also make an announcement before the end of the year. If not both of these major players are likely to have big plans for the New Year, that will make 2016 a very exciting year.

It is also probable that both of these major players have big plans to offer services and products that will draw consumers to their platforms. So it will not be surprising if they both challenge Facebook and Twitter. That would be great news because more choices will provide better opportunities for small businesses and independent operators.

At the same time more and more people are buying products on the internet every single day. In fact, hundreds of millions of consumers all over the world spend billions of dollars buying everything imaginable on the internet. As a result, there has never been a better time to utilize Viral Marketing to do or to start doing business on the Internet; due to advances in software, training, technology, and the power of sharing on social media networks.

3.) FAST START STRATEGIES

Achieve success in any area of life by identifying the optimum strategies and repeating them until they become habits. via Charles J Givens

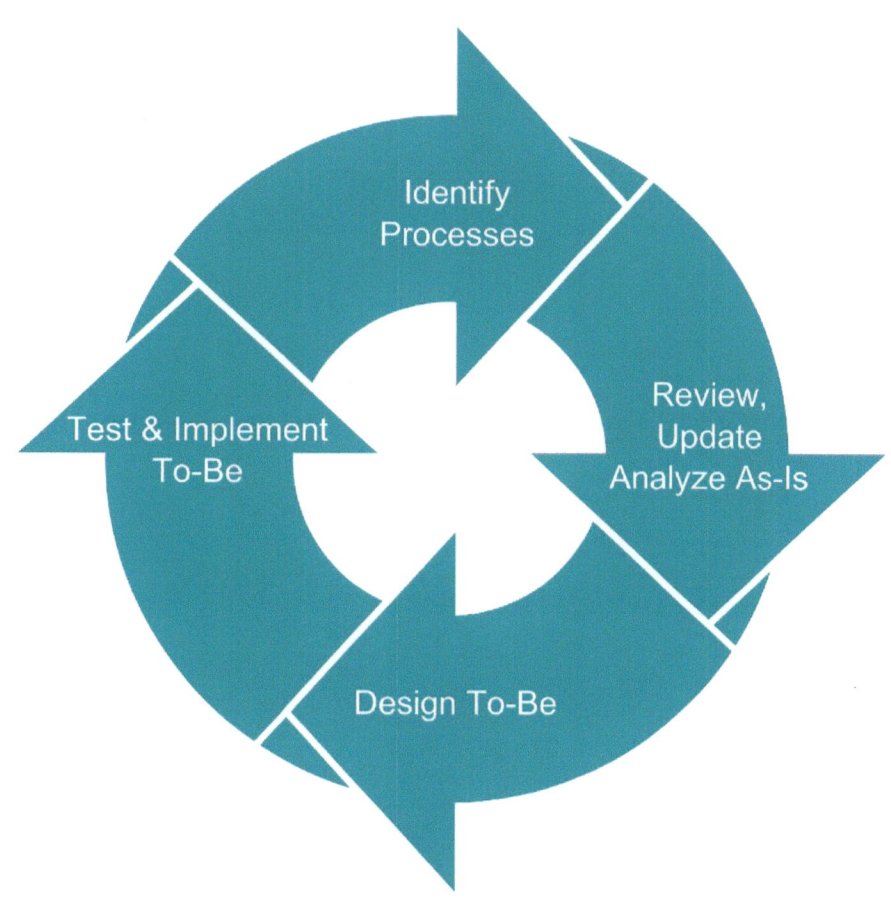

Business Process Reengineering Cycle

This eBook provides several low cost Viral Marketing strategies that have proven to be profitable. These strategies are also the essential elements that are required for any Viral Marketing campaign to be successful. In most cases you can get started today on a very small budget. This eBook also emphasizes that to be successful it is essential to mimic and imitate success. It has been said that if you want to be successful you must tie your rope to the wagon of someone who is already successful.

So the fastest way to come up with your own great business ideas is to look at and study how the most successful people are already doing the things that you are interested in doing. Then you just need to mimic and imitate how they are doing business, but find a new twist, do it better, or update what they are doing to start your own business. That method is a tried and proven strategy to give you the great potential to be successful.

Ideally, many successful Internet Marketers have started successful online businesses for less than $100 by using Viral Marketing. Of course if you want to implement a Viral Marketing campaign that requires a 10 page website and a promotional video that requires professional camera work, a live demonstrator, a live narrator, and a script writer most likely you will need to spend thousands of dollars. On the other hand 1 webpage that is professionally developed can be just as or an even more effective sales tool than a 10 page site your website visitors may not take time to look at.

Usually things that go viral are short and to the point. For effective Viral Marketing 1 webpage is likely to be better than a professionally developed 10 page site. In addition, it is relatively easy to learn how to produce your own videos these days. Almost everyone walks around with the technology to produce professional videos in their pockets these days.

James Wedmore who is one of the top Internet Marketers on Youtube just recently shared the fact that he produced his latest video without a camera by using his cellphone. So the most powerful technology is available and probably in your hand or pocket and you can get started right now. Matter of fact you can even get the advanced training and all the additional tools and resources you need, to setup your very own Video Production Agency very inexpensively. It is called Instant Video Machine and it will enable you to produce high quality videos for businesses you can find right in your local area at:

http://blog.paladinmovies.com/instantvideo

There is no doubt that people love video so that makes it the ultimate Viral Marketing tool, but don't overlook eBooks. Because they can be created quickly for very little cost and they can also generate huge profits. eBooks always have and obviously always be big sellers. Book stores are closing and people still like, want, and need the best most up to date information.

The fact that you can get information in your possession in a matter of seconds makes eBooks the big winner over physical paper paperback books. The down side to selling eBooks are:

 A) People buying them and asking for refunds

 B) People illegally sharing and giving away and selling your work

But of course there are downsides to every business, but fortunately there is no loss on refunds for an eBook compared to a physical book that can no longer be sold as new. In addition, the Viral Marketing strategy provided later in this eBook flips the switch and encourages people to download and share your eBook for FREE to increase your profits!

Ideally, once you have done your research to find out what the best selling books are you can buy the Private Label Rights (PLR) and even find some great FREE

PLR eBooks that are dated then update and revise them in 7 days or less, if you are a fairly good writer from a very reliable and reputable company such as: http://resellrightsbargain.net/ Best of all you will be able to make money without even selling your eBook by making it a Viral Marketing eBook!

Even if you have no interest in writing an eBook or you are not a good writer you can still become a great Viral Marketer, and make money by joining and promoting an affiliate program that has a 2 tiered payment structure. In general affiliate programs are a great way to get started in Viral Marketing. Basically, companies setup affiliate programs to pay commissions to independent sales reps. The best programs do not charge a fee to become an affiliate, and they have 2 tiered payment structures.

2 tiered affiliate programs pay you an over ride commission on referral sales and/or if you recruit other sub-affiliates who make sales. A great example of an affiliate program with a 2 tiered payment structure for a product that people like, want, and need is the affiliate program for Facebook Traffic Ninja Pro (FBTN Pro): http://www.fbtrafficninja.com/trinity-jv/ People like getting better results for the ads they run on Facebook, they want more website clicks, and most people

need to save money on the cost of advertising. FBTN Pro does all that by enabling people who advertise on Facebook to get website clicks for as little as or less than 1 cent each. You can get more info at: http://www.fbtrafficninja.com/pro

You can also signup as an affiliate at: http://www.fbtrafficninja.com/trinity-jv/ The good part about promoting an affiliate program is there is no need to write books or develop your own products. All you need to do is refer people and/or send traffic to the company's affiliate website to sell their products to get paid. If you are interested in learning how to be or become a better affiliate marketer you can also click on our affiliate link to get a 30 day trial on some of the best training that

is available for ONLY $1.00 at: http://blog.paladinmovies.com/rrazor/affiliorama

OK, lets get back to creating a Viral Marketing eBook and the advantages for sharing and giving it away compared to selling your eBook. The main objective for creating a Viral Marketing eBook is so that it will be shared and for people to spread it around the Internet quickly and virally.

The objective is not for you to make you money on the front end. Ideally, you just want other people giving it away to as many people as possible. Why? Because the inside of your book is full of your affiliate links to your products or the products of other people, especially if the other products have a 2 tiered affiliate program. Then every time someone shares and/or gives away your eBook more people will see your affiliate links. This will increase opportunities for you to make sales virally, without you having to spend money on additional advertising.

This eBook is new so it is too soon to tell if it will go viral (Be Sure To Share The Love & Make it Go Viral) but a proven example that this method of Viral Marketing is extremely effective are eBooks by Yanik Silver. He created 2 marketing eBooks that spread virally around the Internet. To do that he gave everyone who purchased his ebooks for $19 or $17 (depending on the book) the rights to sell it or give it away to their customers. As as a result thousands of people starting selling it and promoting it all over the Internet. As far as I know Yank Silver may still be earning money from those eBooks, and he became a famously well known Internet Marketer.

4.) How To Come Up With An Idea For A Viral eBook

Great ideas get even better when you share them. via Loesje

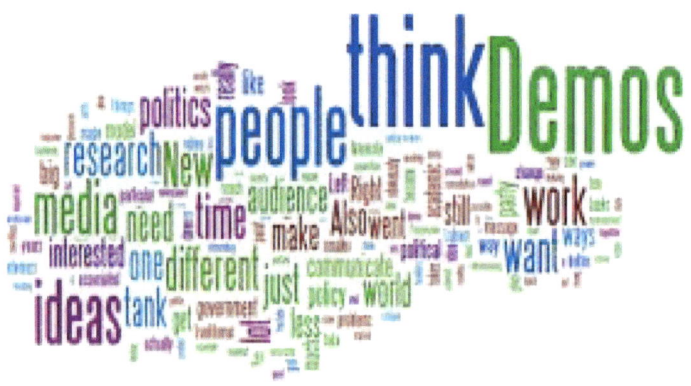

1. Coming up with ideas for your eBook isn't hard.

The main thing to remember is that your eBook must be based on what people like, want, and need. Then it will be a much easier to setup your own affiliate program and go viral. Or to get started quickly you can base your eBook on and promote an affiliate program that has a 2 tiered payment structure. But an easy way to come up with ideas to write your own eBook is to look at and mimic what kind of eBooks others are already selling successfully, then provide new updated, and/or additional information that people like, want, and need.

2. Professional Tools For Viral Marketing

All serious professional Internet Marketers have their own domain (website name) and a website and/or blog. One option is to choose a fairly short domain name that describes the content of your eBook. Although we chose a domain name that allows us to promote any new product we want such as: http://highlightzone.biz/retargetrazor

3. You also need a good reliable web hosting company with 24/7 technical

support.

If your site goes down you must be able to contact someone to get it back up quickly. Currently we use Godaddy which is a little pricey, and recently I have heard from reliable sources that Bluehost is just as good. You can use our affiliate link to get a special price offer on a domain name and hosting at: http://blog.paladinmovies.com/bluehost

4. Next You Need An Autoresponder

You will need an autoresponder so that you can allow people to signup and download your free eBook. FYI 92 to 98% of people don't purchase on their first visit to any webpage so the best way not to lose potential sales is to allow people to signup for your free eBook, that is monetized with your affiliate links.

If you are just starting and do not have an autoresponder you can signup and use www.mailchimp.com for free until you get your first 2000 subscribers, then Getresponse may be cheaper when you have more that 2000 subscribers. PLUS you can use our affiliate link to get a 30 day free trial at: http://blog.paladinmovies.com/getresponse

5. You Also Need A Credit card processor

The most popular affiliate networks that work with Paypal, which is the best processor for major credit cards are Clickbank and Jvzoo, but we recently moved to: http://blog.paladinmovies.com/zaxaaThis step was an easy decision for us to make because Zaxaa charges the lowest fees and they have a new state of the art network, that is easy use with responsive tech support. Best of all Zaxaa also has a 2 tiered affiliate program and will pay us for using their network! Check out the video and see for yourself why we made the move to Zaxaa: https://www.youtube.com/watch?v=eU6E-jy28QA

6. eBook Software

It is best to create your book in PDF format so that pc and mac users can read it. Mac users can't read some formats so that is the main reason why it is best to use PDF for your eBook format. You can easily create your PDF eBook with: http://www.dopdf.com/ We use it because it is also easy to install and using it is a no brainer. PLUS it is FREE and it works with all word processors.

FYI we use OpenOffice because it seems to be more much more responsive than

MS Word. OpenOffice is very dependable and almost always recovers open

documents that are usually lost if a laptop shuts down due to a low battery. It even

recovers documents if there is an unexpected pc crash or shut down. MS Word

does not always recover documents that have been unexpectedly closed and lost.

PLUS did I mention that it is FREE: http://www.openoffice.org/welcome

Although, if you already have an eBook or time dated info you need to share

quickly you can revise your work using the suggestions in this eBook for Viral

Marketing. Then when you have transformed your eBook you can upload and

distribute it freely from Google Drive or DropBox, and maybe http://filehippo.com

which is or used to be free.

Also remember the objective is to give away and share to promote your Viral

Marketing eBook. The more it is shared the more commissions you are likely to

earn from the affiliate links that are included for products people like, want, and

need. And be sure to clearly state in the front of your eBook that the reader can

freely share it and/or signup to become an affiliate for the programs in your

eBook, then share and earn commissions.

Another important thing that all Pro Internet Marketers do is to use an autoresponder to create a "Subscribe To My Updates" section in your eBook to earn commissions and generate leads automatically. if you are just getting started you can use MailChimp: www.mailchimp.com or if you have more than 2000 subscribers already on your list then Getresponse may be the best option: http://blog.paladinmovies.com/getresponse

Once you have created your eBook and uploaded it, and it is ready to be shared, you will need to write a salesletter for your eBook. Even though this can be the easiest part of the whole process the best advice is to spend as much time and care on writing the salesletter as you did writing the eBook itself. This process is usually easy because the subject matter of your eBook should be popular, if you followed the suggestions in this eBook for creating your Viral Marketing eBook.

5.) VIRAL MARKETING TIPS

The aim of marketing is to know and understand the customer so well the product or service fits him and sells itself. via Peter Drucker

The first Viral Marketing Tip is to always mimic and imitate success. So to create a Viral Marketing eBook all you need to do is go Amazon to see what the top selling books are, or just go to google and type in "the most popular (subject of your eBook) eBooks for 2015". Google will return the websites of the most popular eBooks for you to review and select the most compelling webpages for you to copy the text and revise as your own.

The next step is to revise the best text from 3 or more of popular webpages then most likely your salesletter will be unique and outstanding. Probably a professional copywriter would charge you thousands of dollars to do this for you. Once you have a great salesletter obviously you can also use it and your eBook cover to make a quick promo webpage for your eBook.

Another Tip is that Viral Marketing strategies can also be used to increase sales for products on and offline. Ideally, Viral Marketing strategies can be used by small businesses, non profits, independent professionals, and talent to economically promote products and projects online. Any professional who has a products or service for sale right now can use our Zaxaa affiliate link to signup for a 30 day FREE trial of Zaxaa Deluxe services to recruit and manage affiliates to promote projects and/or sales reps to increase sales: http://blog.paladinmovies.com/zaxaa

The final Tip for now is that the best affiliates and sales reps are most interested in promoting and selling top quality products for the highest price. As a result, the best affiliates and reps expect a minimum of 50% on products that sell for less than $100. Increasingly affiliates are offered 100% commission on products selling for less than $25. Of course these are usually digital products so the product owner incurs no loss. On the other hand you are very likely to find affiliates and reps who will sell a high priced ticket product that costs $1000 for 30% commission.

Also depending on the quality and popularity of the product affiliates may even promote a $1000 product for 10% commission. Most importantly don't be like most average old pre-digital style companies, that take the referral sales and recruit the customers of their sales affiliates and reps. Setup a 2 tiered payment plan that encourages affiliates and reps to ask for referrals and recruit more affiliates and sales reps for your company or project. In the long term you gain loyalty from affiliates and reps that increases profits.

6.) Advertising & Promoting Your eBook

"Doing business without advertising is like winking at a girl in the dark. You know what you are doing but nobody else does." via Steuart Henderson Britt

OK now we will get back on track. To be completely honest I must admit that lately we are spending just as much advertising money on Twitter ads as we are spending on Facebook ads, because Twitter has delivered excellent results. Although the reason we started advertising on Twitter is because doing business and advertising on Facebook can be very similar to trying to walk on egg shells without cracking them on a crowded beach. Possibly most Internet Marketers who run ads on Facebook may be afraid to openly tell you that, but in private you would probably get the truth.

But we have a dilemma when it comes to Facebook due to the phenomenal 1 cent per website click results we get when running ads on Facebook. You can see the *Live Proof* video of our phenomenal results on Youtube at:

https://youtu.be/eMG7MrPikC0 No doubt you will agree it is too quick and easy to get cheap website clicks to pass up the opportunity.

So we will continue to use the Facebook Traffic Ninja Pro (FBTN Pro) method to get cheap website clicks: http://www.fbtrafficninja.com/pro and also the New RetargetRazor Pro: http://highlightzone.biz/retargetrazorpro software that will be released on the 17th of November to promote and advertise this on Facebook.

Affiliates Are Invited To Join The Technological Revolution & Promote The RetargetRazor Pro Launch! Get Your link to promote this 2 Tiered Affiliate Program *NOW* at: http://highlightzone.biz/rrprojv/

Overall, Viral Marketing works best when using all of the major social networks and promotional opportunities that are available. As a result, we are running ads to give away our eBook, and also to find affiliates who will share our Viral Marketing eBook to earn commissions. In addition, we are also going to post announcements to the 50+ Facebook groups that we belong to promote our eBook to go viral.

Posting announcements to Facebook groups is a very viable strategy everyone should be using, since if done properly it is a powerful method to promote a product to go viral. Best of all there is no cost to implement this strategy and it requires little time to accomplish. We are also going to test variations on a couple of old no cost Viral Marketing strategies.

Although both strategies can be implemented without cost they do require some serious work compared to the ease of posting to Facebook groups. But the work may be well worth the effort because of the profit potential, and the easy startup because no website is required.

The first strategy is to find highly popular ezines that are targeting people who may be interested in your eBook, because these ezines already have the customers you and we want. To do that I typed ezine directories into google and got what looks like great results. The best result we found might be the search site at: http://www.ezinefinder.com/search.html This site may cut the time to find ezine publishers who advertise eBooks and products related to Viral Marketing or products related to your eBook.

The next strategy requires contacting website and blog owners. Both strategies require approaching ezine and site owners in a particular way to get access to their site visitors for free. Ezine and Site owners normally sell products in exchange for 50% commission on the sales made. In our case the eBook is free so we must emphasize to ezine and site owners that they get 50% commission and 2nd tier bonuses when they signup as affiliates.

On the other hand finding website and blog owners who are willing to become our joint venture partners and share our eBook with their customer base was not the expected quick and easy task using the usual method of searching google for keywords related our eBook title. Now after performing a quick test my thinking is that I may get faster and better results for contacting website and blog owners by using Twitter. To document and share the results we will produce a short video and a Case Study. To get FREE access just Follow & Tweet: @GorillaShooting

Add me to the Viral Marketing List

7.) CONCLUSION

Determination fuels the effort to take it to a logical conclusion. It is firmness in attitude & approach, to never to give up. via Dr Anil Kr Sinha

So far the most accurate definition for Viral Marketing seems to be, "*Viral Marketing is the rapid sharing of an idea or message, that is intended to encourage support of the idea, or a project, and/or to encourage the purchase of services, or products*"

Viral Marketing is a phenom, which has converged with technological advances, that provides unprecedented opportunities for small businesses, independent professionals, non profits, talent, and also the masses who have a smartphone. No doubt the media and other conglomerates are trembling, because the masses have never before had access to such unlimited communications power.

Ideally, technological development is continuing to rapidly transfer the power of mass communication from the media conglomerates to individualized massive multimedia interaction. It is no longer a seller's market because buyers now have multiple choices of communications media and social networks. The only way the conglomerates like Clear Channel can regain control would be to shut the Internet down and ban the development of new PDAs, cellphones, and ipads, that could probably replace the Internet and create a new unregulated network.

Fortunately that scenario seems unlikely to happen and as you have read in this eBook it is relatively quick and easy to create a Viral Marketing eBook. Although a Viral Marketing eBook is usually shared freely it can be used to promote projects and also to sell digital products; and/or even to sell high priced products, on or offline by recruiting affiliates. We have only scratched the surface of the potential for utilizing Viral Marketing. The objective has been to provide practical information, resources, and access to technology that can be used right now.

There are many other great ways Viral Marketing can be used, that have not been covered in this eBook, but ideally it has provided some food for thought and motivated you to take action. Because there are probably thousands of ways to use Viral Marketing to communicate ideas, promote projects, and increase profits. Remember that the most Essential strategy for utilizing Viral Marketing is to mimic and imitate the success of others.

The most important Tip is to start now. Technology is developing rapidly, change is imminent, and today's opportunity will be gone tomorrow. So make a plan and make it happen one step at a time. Remember the search for perfection in the perfect time to start, the perfect circumstances, the perfect product, or whatever perfect thing usually leads to inaction and going no where. Get started today go forward and be a work in progress, that gets better and closer to perfection as you achieve results.

Lastly and most importantly I must give thanks and appreciation for all of the great information, graphics, software, training, documents, and the other excellent works that have been freely shared on the Internet. It provides substantiated proof that there are people on the world willing to put in the work required to make the world a better place. This eBook could not have been written, published, and shared with you without them.

Some of the best things in life are still truly available on the Internet. Be sure to join the Viral Marketing List on Twitter to get the Video documentation and Case Study of results on this eBook promotion & Updates On More Great Resources!

For Access & Updates Tweet: @GorillaShooting Add me to the Viral Marketing List

8.) Use My Favorite eBook Titles For FREE
Be Free Unleash The Creative Beast That Is Inside Of You!

1. How to create short reports and sell them online.

2. 54 ways to make more money with affiliate programs.

3. Beginners Guide to Internet Marketing.

4. How to Find Untapped Markets with Pay Per Click Search Engines.

5. How to become a super affiliate on a budget.

6. Ezine advertising made easy.

7. Amazing case stories of how people make their fortunes online.

8. How to setup your own affiliate program on a budget.

9. Free advertising guide.

10. How to use free downloads to get thousands of website visitors.

11. Create Your Own Viral Marketing Campaign.

12. The Insider Secrets to Affiliate Marketing Success.

13. How to make your fortune online with your favorite hobbies.

14. How to Make & Sell Your Own Lava Lamps Online.

15. How to Make Home Made Soaps For Profit.

16. How To Become A Pro DJ.

17. How To Make Money Online With Recipe eBooks.

18. How to start your own Internet radio station.

19. How to Start Your Own Online Music Shop.

20. How to Make Money with Your Love Of Music.

21. How to Start Your Own Online Travel Agency.

22. How to Make Money with Your Love Of Golf.

23. How to Make Money with Your Love Of Traveling.

24. How to become a profitable freelance writer.

25. 52 top US bed and breakfasts in the US.

26. Luxury Travel for the Rich and Famous ON A BUDGET!

27. The Complete Guide to Christian Travel.

28. The Complete Guide to Adventure Travel.

29. How to get the best ski resorts for the lowest price.

30. The Complete Guide to Student And Budget World Travel.

31. The Great Accommodations Price War.

32. Take the Best Golfing Holiday In The World for A Bargain Price!

33. Single travel for the 30's and under.

34. How to Buy A Used Car Without Getting Ripped Off.

35. 1001 Unusual Baby Names.

36. 101 Money Saving Techniques.

37. Quick and Easy Microwavable Recipes.

38. How to Throw the Ultimate Bachelor & Bachelorette Parties.

39. How to Putt Like the Pros.

40. How to become a highly paid golf caddy

41. Change The World In 2016

42. Where There Is A Will A Way Can Always Be Made.

43. Each One Must Teach 10.

44. Please Steal These Ideas For Change.

45. Some Of The Best Things In Life Are Still FREE On The Internet!

9.) FREE RESOURCES

"Some Of The Best Things In Life Are Still FREE On The Internet!"

7 Zip: http://7-zip.org (free download)
An open source, free alternative to WinZip.

Audacity: http://audacity.sourceforge.net (free download)
An open source software used for recording & editing audio files.

AVG: http://free.avg.com (free download)
Anti-virus and anti-spyware protection.

BrowserShots: http://browsershots.org (free online tool)
Use this site to view how your website look in various browsers.

CamStudio: http://camstudio.org (free download)
Lets you record all screen & audio activity on your computer and create video files.

CCleaner: http://ccleaner.com (free download)
Removes unused files from your pc allowing Windows to run faster and freeing up space.

Color Cop: http://colorcop.net (free online tool)
A mulch-purpose color picker - great for web designers and programmers.

Down For Everyone: http://downforeveryoneorjustme.com (free online tool) Is your site down? Use this tool to see if your website is down for other people.

DupeFree: http://dupefreepro.com (free download)
Quickly check for duplicate content & LSI keywords.

Evernote: http://evernote.com (free download)
Scan your notes, receipts, etc … it will OCR the content, space it, and make it searchable.

FileZilla: http://filezilla-project.org (free download)
Open source FTP program for uploading files to your host.
Firefox: http//mozilla.com/firefox (free download)

Alternate web browser.

GIMP: http://gimp.org (free download) An open source program used to create & edit - free alternative to Photoshop.

Give Away Of The Day: http://giveawayoftheday.com (free download) Unique site that offers you a free license digital product daily.

Kompozer: http://kompozer.net (free download)
An easy to use WYSIWYG HTML editor.

NicheBot Classic: http://nichebotclassic.com (free online tool)
Online keyword research tool helps you target the correct keywords.

Open Office: http://openoffice.org (free download) FREE Open source office software - word processing, spreadsheets, databases, presentations & best alternative to MS Word.

OSWD: http://oswd.org/ (free downloads)
Open Source Web Design offers free web design templates.

PDF995: http://pdf995.com (free download)
Use this tool to easily convert files to PSD format.

PDF to Word Converter: http://pdftoword.com (free online tool)
Easily create editable Word Doc files from PDF content – for legit purposes only.

Pixie: http://nattyware.com/pixie.php (free download)
Great for web designers - just point to a color and discover the code value for that color.

Roboform: http://roboform.com (free download)
Easily & safely manage your passwords.

ScreenHunter: http://wisdom-soft.com/sh/sh_free.htm (free download) Software that allows you to "capture" any part of your desktop, a window or full screen.

Skype: http://skype.com (free download)
Make free calls over the internet to other people on Skype.

Textpad: http://textpad.com (free download) A powerful text editor. I personally like Textpad for editing HTML code.

VLC Media Player: http://videolan.org/vlc (free download)
Media player capable of reading most audio and video formats.

WordPress Help Sheets And Resources: http://1stwebdesigner.com/wordpress
23 extremely helpful WordPress help sheets and resources.